What Christians Have Always Believed

Words and Pictures by
Maxine McDonald

With gratitude to Dr. John Adair and Dr. John Hannah,
who introduced me to the saints of old,

and to Mom and Dad, who have taught and modeled
what Christians believe for forty years together.

Copyright © 2022 by Unlikely Publications Global, LLC.
www.unlikelypublicationsglobal.com

ISBN: 978-1-7374045-6-9

Maybe even here!

There are Christians all over the place,
So many millions they're quite hard to trace.
In mountains and valleys
And dark city alleys—
Who knows?—there might even be Christians in space!

Christians live all over here.

And here!

If thousands of years have already gone by
Since Jesus went up on the clouds in the sky,
How can we be sure if
Our faith is secure if
It's just word of mouth on which we all rely?

What's *worse* is that Christians don't always agree.
Sometimes we argue. There's no guarantee
That what one Christian claims
Won't go right up in flames
When the next one explains what he's come to believe.

But that doesn't mean that there's no way to know
That we *still* teach what Jesus taught so long ago.
We debate what's unclear,
But the core we hold dear.
Our faith stands on more than just some status quo.

I hope that your worries will soon be relieved.
We still have the truth the disciples received.
Because God made a way
We can still know today
The things *all* Christians *everywhere always* believed.

Traditional Theology

Jesus's best friend was John.
John took the teaching that Jesus passed on.
And he taught it to Polycarp (What a cool name!).
Polycarp's teaching was still just the same
As what John said, and Jesus told John what to say.
Down through the decades, truth passed on that way
From one generation right onto the next
(Though some of the names aren't what we might expect).
Here our American tongues might betray us—
Polycarp's student was called Irenaeus.

Lots of God's people with hard names to say
Wrote letters and books we can still read today,
Like Cyril, and Clement, Augustine, Ignatius,
Three Cappadocians, and one Athanasius.
If we're ever not sure what we're hearing is true,
We go back to these sources and look there for clues.
We call it *Tradition*. The truth was passed down
Through reliable people who we study now.
These heroes protected the truth they received—
Things that *all* Christians *everywhere always* believed.

There aren't a lot of Christians here, but you can find a few if you know where to look.

Could some be living here?

Did <u>you</u> think church history's only for grown-ups?
In fact, you can learn it no matter your size.
Want to know what the ancient believers have shown us?
Church history's easy to learn if it rhymes.

An Apology for Theology

Do you know what theology is?
I'll give you a hint if you're stuck:
It's a word to describe
What goes on inside
The Church when a question comes up.

When somebody says, "I don't understand!"
Or, "This teaching just doesn't make sense,"
Then we turn to God's Word
And the truths that we've learned.
The discussions can get kinda tense.

Theology is a collection of answers
To questions that people have asked
That the Church organized
And then categorized
And wrote down so those answers would last.

No one sat down and came up with a list
Of ideas to argue about.
They'd just teach and contend,
Explain and defend,
As people had questions and doubts.

If *you* have a question, then there's a good chance
That someone has asked it before.
The answer they found
Might help you right now,
And that's what theology's for.

The Church's theology grows and develops,
And sometimes we still disagree.
But the core doesn't change,
Because God stays the same.
It's what *all* Christians *everywhere always* believed.

Some Christians live in places that are pretty hard to get to, like way up here.

Could a Christian live here?

Orthodoxy and Orthopraxy

Ortho*DOX*y means you believe what is true.
Ortho*PRAX*y refers to right things that you do.
If your doxy's all right but your praxy's gone wonky,
Or your praxy's right on but your doxy's all zonky,
Try hard as you might, you'll for sure be off sync
Between how you behave and the thoughts that you think.
We must both know *and* do—or else God will be grieved—
The things *all* Christians *everywhere always* believed.

Some Christians go to church in boats!

Some say theology's only for grown-ups.
In fact, you can learn it no matter your size.
You can understand, with God's help, what he's shown us.
Theology's easy to learn if it rhymes.

You might find one in a house like this.

Let's Add Theology Proper into the Hopper

One of the first things the Church had to solve
Was how to explain that we worship one God
Who exists in three Persons, the great Three-in-One:
The Father, the Spirit, and Jesus (the Son).*
It's the core of our faith, and it has to be true
For the gospel to save people like me and you.

It took three hundred years for the Church to decide
On a word we could use as a way to describe
That God is three Persons and that they're all one:
The *Trinity* (Father, and Spirit, and Son).
A man named Tertullian thought up that term,
And it's an important one for you to learn.

The Father and Spirit and Son aren't the same.
They're three separate Persons, the Bible makes plain.
The Three are all equal, eternal, united.
They can be distinguished but never divided.
There's only one God. Let's be clear about that.
If it's hard to imagine, you're on the right track.

*When we talk of the Trinity, you'll often hear it
As Father, then Son, and *then* Holy Spirit.
The Son is the Second, the Spirit is Third,
And that is the order I would have preferred,
But it turns out that Spirit's a hard word to rhyme,
So I've switched up the order here some of the time.

We can't understand God. No surprise there!
There's only one of him, so nothing compares.
Some people use pictures to help to explain
How the Persons are different and how they're the same.
But every picture has some fatal flaw.
No metaphor captures the nature of God.

The Father is God, and God is just one.
God also includes both the Spirit and Son.
Jesus is God, every bit, all the way,
Not "sort of" or "almost," as some tried to say.
The Spirit is just as much God as the Son
And the Father is too, but remember, they're one.

Don't get too distracted with how it all works.
The Bible is quite clear in what it asserts.
We know that there's only one God. No debate.
He exists as three Persons who interrelate.
Though the concept is hard for our minds to conceive,
It's what *all* Christians *everywhere always* believed.

In some places, you have to walk a long, long way to find another Christian.

And Now For Bibliology:
God's Written-Down Theology

Are there Christians under all this snow?!?

Have Christians always read the Bible
And had morning quiet times?
Did they mark and highlight pages?
Did their Bibles look like mine?

Would you be shocked if I told you they didn't?
That no one had personal Bibles back then?
Most early Christians would never have touched one
Except for some scholars and very rich men.

One generation explained to the next
The really important things that they would need
To faithfully follow the teachings of Jesus
So people could learn them if they couldn't read.

Well, in that case, where'd it come from?
How can we be sure it's true?
Who decided it should have the
Sixty-six books we include?

Do you remember the big word *Tradition*?
The Old and New Testament books were passed down.
As they were collected and written and read from,
The Church would make copies and pass them around.

They knew which books were God's true revelation
And which were just regular writings by men.
There wasn't a lot of discussion about it
'Cause Christians all mostly agreed on it then.

Each church had *some* parts of the Bible and shared them
With everyone else, but it took quite some time
'Til *all* of the books got to *all* of the churches
And formed into Bibles like yours and like mine.

You could bump into one
in an elevator...

How can we be sure the copies
Don't mix up the things they say?
Are there mistakes or missing pieces?
Can we trust them still today?

The Church recognizes what we call the Canon:
The sixty-six books that we know are from God.
Because he is perfect and truthful and holy,
The words of his Bible can't have any flaws.

We still have access to really old copies
Of all of the books so that we can compare
What our Bibles say now to those much older versions
And see that the copies were made with great care.

Well, then, let's be super thankful
For a Bible we can read.
That's how we can know for sure what
All Christians everywhere always believed.

...or on a bus.

Hamartiology: The Saddest of Theologies

Sin is not doing what God says to do.
I sin quite often. I'm sure you do, too.
No matter how hard we may try to be good,
We still never please God like we know we should.

Before we were born, we *already* had sin.
We've no cure for the terrible trouble we're in.
Because Adam sinned, we have guilt, fear, and shame.
We add on our own sin, so we share the blame.

A man named Pelagius said, "That's not true.
We're not dead in our sins. We're alive and can choose
To be perfect if we would just try hard enough.
Grace might be helpful, but it's up to us."

The Church had a meeting and studied God's Word.
They prayed and debated and thought and conferred.
Augustine from Hippo—I promise that's true!—
Finally stood up and spoke for the group:

"Pelagius, you've made an awful mistake.
There's no cure for our sin except for God's grace."
That's how God helped the Church to defend and to teach
Something *all* Christians *everywhere always* believed.

Some Christians don't even live on land!
They build houses on stilts, right in the ocean.

And Now Soteriology: Our Saving Grace Theology

We talked about sin and how we need God's grace.
Let's think for a bit about how they relate.
Our sin is *so* bad that we have no hope,
No way to remove it, no way we can cope.
No choices we make, no battles we win
Can cure the *impossible* problem of sin.

So what should we do? Do we just give up?
I would if God hadn't shown grace to us.
The way God can offer us sinners salvation
Is by an exchange that we call *imputation*:
    Adam's sin was imputed to you.
    And so you are guilty and I'm guilty, too.
    Our sin was imputed to Christ.
    That's how he can promise us eternal life.
    Christ's righteousness was imputed to us.
    And *that* is the *best* news that there *ever* was.

Some Christians have a great view!

Our sins are the reason that Jesus Christ died.
And then on the third day he came back to life!
It happened exactly like Scripture had said.
We can trade in our sin and have life now instead.
　　And *why* did he do it? Did somebody make him?
　　Has anyone ever *deserved* this salvation?
　　Not even a little. Not even a smidge.
　　There isn't a reason God did what he did—
　　No reason at all that he saved me and you—
　　Except that he loves us and *he* wanted to.

When we were rebellious and ugly and mean,
God made the decision that he would redeem.
All *we* have to do is believe it by faith
And receive the free gift of God's undeserved grace.
That is the gospel, and that is the key
To what *all* Christians *everywhere always* believed.

There could be lots of them in a big city like this.

Did you think that Christians could only be grown-ups?
You can become one no matter your size.
Just pray and thank God for the grace that he's shown us.
Repent and believe in the Lord Jesus Christ.

In some places, there have been
Christians for hundreds of years.

In other places,
people are just now
hearing about Jesus
for the very first time.

Our Christology: God's Great Anomaly

When Jesus was here, there was lots of discussion
Of whether he really was God.
Some said he was, and some said he wasn't.
Some called him Messiah. Some called him a fraud.
But once Jesus died and was then resurrected,
All Christians agreed he's divine.
It was hard to explain from a human perspective
How he could be both God and man at one time.

     But here is the main thing I want you to know:
     The earliest Christians believed he was both.

Jesus is human, one hundred percent.
That's why he got tired and hungry and sad.
It's how he could take on all *our* human sin
And why he understands the temptations we have.
And Jesus is God—the Lord Jesus Christ—
The only redeemer that there could have been.
He *had* to be God for his one sacrifice
To totally cancel out everyone's sin.

     One person, two natures—how could that be?
     It's one of the great Christian mysteries.

God deserves to be worshipped...

Nobody else could fulfill God's great plan
Because nobody else can be both God and man.
Nobody else could redeem us from sin.
Nobody else who *ever* has been
Could take on our sin as a man who could die
And pay infinite debt with his infinite life.
He's one-of-a-kind, and he's God's *only* Son:
The God-man incarnate, two natures in one.*

...in sunshiny tropical places...

All Christians *everywhere* *always* believed
That Jesus is an anomaly.

*He's the God-man now and always
So the Church made up a catchphrase
That means he's both God and human:
It's the *hypostatic union.*

The Church's Own Theology
Is Called Ecclesiology

All Christians *everywhere always* believed
That God saves us each individually,
But he doesn't want us to stay on our own.
He groups us together so we're not alone.
We call a gathering of Christians a *church*.
We worship together and then we disperse.

...and frigid arctic places too.

You *might* think of church as a place that you go
Each Sunday to worship with people you know.
You listen to sermons, you pray, and you sing.
That's part of the Church, but it's not the whole thing.
The Church is the people of God, not a place—
All Christians *everywhere*, saved by God's grace.

Some meet in buildings with steeples on top.
Some in cathedrals, others in shops.
Some meet in malls. Some rent the Y.
Some meet in schools, and some meet outside.
Some meet online, or even on Zoom.
Most churches this week will be in living rooms.

The Church is the visible body of Christ.
You join in the body by getting baptized.
Together we celebrate Jesus's death
By taking communion with wine and with bread.
Churches look different from one to the next,
But we're all united—north, south, east, and west.

The Church isn't perfect and sometimes we won't
Act like Jesus would want—at least I know *I* don't!
We're learning together to act like we should
And growing together like God said we would.
We're Jesus's bride, his treasured possession,
And *lots* of the Church is already in heaven.

God promised that one day his Church will include
People from everywhere so he can prove
That he's worthy of worship from every tribe,
Language, and culture that he has designed.
So God sent us out to the *whole* world to be
The keepers and teachers of what we believe.

And Now for Some Chronology: Let's Tackle Eschatology

Have you noticed that even though Jesus has come,
     People still sin?
     And we still cry.
     Bullies are mean.
     Everyone dies.
     People get hurt.
     And we get sick.
     Our broken world
     Still isn't fixed.

Remember that Jesus's story's not done.
     Someday he'll judge.
     Someday he'll reign
     And heal every hurt
     And break every chain.
     He's coming back
     And he'll raise the dead.
     He *will* fix it all.
     He just hasn't yet.

God will fulfill every promise he made.
     So don't despair,
     Bad as it gets.
     We know the ending.
     This isn't it.
     We wait with hope
     From now until then.
     We know that he's coming,
     We just don't know when.

Remember, all the Christians in all these places have a whole lot in common...

Christians have always lived in the last days.
That's nothing new.
God didn't say
Which of the last days
Will be the *last* day.
Get ready now.
And never forget,
Eschatology
Tells us the key word is *yet*.

(even here!)

You will find as you study and listen and read
That lots of good Christians have all disagreed
On the details of what's gonna happen and when—
The order and timeline of how things will end.
But Christians have always agreed on the fact
That Jesus is King, and the King's coming back.

It's good to consider the different views,
But remember, whichever main system you choose,
When Jesus *does* come, we'll *all* fall to our knees
And *all* Christians *everywhere* are going to be *astonished.**
Then we'll worship forever—sinless and free—
The Savior who gives us the faith to believe.

*Surprised?

...even though it might not
look like it at first glance.

What's New and What's True

Always be careful that you don't confuse
A thought that sounds new
With a fact that is true.
The latest and greatest idea to come through
Deserves careful thinking, but that's not your cue
To believe it just 'cause it has interested you.
That's how wrong thinking sometimes started and grew.
If you've stumbled into
A strange worldview,
Try to spot and undo
All the parts that aren't true
But *seemed* right all packaged up shiny and new.
The truth is not new,
So don't misconstrue
An interesting thought that you hear on the news
Or a line from a book or an interview
As the next greatest thing that we *all* should now do.
But don't *overdo*
And scorn *everything* new.
Sometimes we need a fresh point of view.
A thought that seems new
Can sometimes be true
If it's actually old, but has been renewed
With more modern words that might *sound* new to you.

What matters is not if a thought *seems* brand-new.
What matters is whether that thought tells the truth.
So don't think it until you are sure through and through
That it matches the things that the Church always knew.
And if it won't match, well, then don't be deceived.
Trust what *all* Christians *everywhere always* believed.

Amen!

9 781737 404569